Jr. Graphic African-American History

Harriet Tubman
Conductor of the Underground Railroad

Susan K. Baumann

PowerKiDS press

New York

Published in 2014 by The Rosen Publishing Group, Inc.
29 East 21st Street, New York, NY 10010

First Edition

Editor: Joanne Randolph

Book Design: Planman Technologies

Illustrations: Planman Technologies

Library of Congress Cataloging-in-Publication Data

Baumann, Susan K.

  Harriet Tubman : conductor of the Underground Railroad / by Susan K. Baumann.

    pages cm. — (Jr. Graphic African-American History)

  Includes index.

  ISBN 978-1-4777-1312-9 (library binding) — ISBN 978-1-4777-1449-2 (pbk.) — ISBN 978-1-4777-1450-8 (6-pack)

  1. Tubman, Harriet, 1820?-1913—Juvenile literature. 2. Slaves—United States—Biography—Juvenile literature. 3. African American women—Biography—Juvenile literature. 4. Underground Railroad—Juvenile literature. 5. Tubman, Harriet, 1820?-1913—Comic books, strips, etc. 6. Slaves—United States—Biography—Comic books, strips, etc. 7. African American women—Biography—Comic books, strips, etc. 8. Underground Railroad—Comic books, strips, etc. 9. Graphic novels. I. Title.

  E444.T82B39 2014

  973.7'115092—dc23

  [B]

                                        2013009470

Manufactured in the United States of America

CPSIA Compliance Information: Batch #WR5150101RC: For Further Information contact Rosen Publishing,
New York, New York at 1-800-237-9932

Contents

Introduction   3

Main Characters   3

Harriet Tubman: Conductor of the
    Underground Railroad   4

Timeline   22

Glossary   23

Index and Websites   24

Introduction

When she was only 25, Harriet Tubman fled her life as a slave. She found her way to freedom in the North. Over the years, she risked her life to go back to the South leading enslaved people to freedom. Tubman led escaping slaves north on the **Underground Railroad**. This was not an actual railroad. It was a large network of people who helped slaves escape. As slaves moved slowly on their journey to freedom in the North, these people, black and white, provided food and safe shelter to help them along the way. Thousands, perhaps as many as 100,000 slaves, escaped from the South traveling on the Underground Railroad. **Conductors** like Tubman were responsible for moving escaping slaves from one safe house to the next. Tubman alone rescued over 300 enslaved people.

Main Characters

Harriet Tubman (c. 1820–1913) Famed conductor on the Underground Railroad.

Frederick Douglass (1818–1895) A famous black **abolitionist**.

Harriet Greene (c. 1790–1879) Harriet Tubman's mother.

Benjamin Ross (c. 1790–1871) Harriet Tubman's father.

HARRIET TUBMAN: CONDUCTOR OF THE UNDERGROUND RAILROAD

ABOUT 1820, HARRIET TUBMAN WAS BORN IN MARYLAND. AS WITH MANY ENSLAVED PEOPLE, HER EXACT BIRTH DATE IS NOT KNOWN. AT THAT TIME, OWNING SLAVES WAS LEGAL IN MARYLAND.

THIS BABY HAS A HARD LIFE AHEAD OF HER. IT'S GOOD THAT SHE IS HEALTHY AND STRONG.

HARRIET'S **ANCESTORS** HAD BEEN BROUGHT TO AMERICA IN THE 1700S. AFTER THEY ARRIVED, THEY WERE SOLD AS SLAVES.

HARRIET'S PARENTS WERE BENJAMIN ROSS AND HARRIET GREENE. THEY WERE OWNED BY EDWARD BRODAS. SLAVES GREW THE CROPS ON HIS **PLANTATION**.

HARRIET HAD MANY BROTHERS AND SISTERS.

IF YOU TEACH SLAVES TO READ, THEY WILL WANT TO ESCAPE TO A BETTER LIFE.

HARRIET NEVER WENT TO SCHOOL. SLAVE OWNERS DID NOT WANT SLAVES TO BE ABLE TO READ AND WRITE.

WHEN SHE WAS ONLY 5 OR 6, HARRIET WAS FORCED TO START WORKING. SLAVE OWNERS OFTEN LOANED THEIR SLAVES TO OTHERS. HARRIET WAS LOANED OUT TO A NEARBY PLANTATION.

YOU ARE GOING TO WORK FOR A NEW MASTER. YOU MUST WORK HARD.

HARRIET'S JOB WAS TO CHECK ANIMAL TRAPS IN THE RIVER.

THIS WATER IS ICY COLD. I AM GOING TO FREEZE OUT HERE.

HARRIET BECAME VERY SICK. SHE WAS SENT BACK TO HER MASTER'S HOUSE.

YOU ARE SKIN AND BONES. DID THEY NOT FEED YOU ANYTHING?

SOON, HARRIET WAS LOANED TO ANOTHER PLANTATION. SHE TOOK CARE OF THE OWNERS' BABY. HARRIET HAD TO KEEP THE BABY FROM CRYING AT NIGHT. THE BABY'S MOTHER BEAT HARRIET IF THE BABY CRIED.

HUSH, LITTLE BABY, DON'T YOU CRY. YOU HAVE A GOOD LIFE.

DAWN TO DUSK, EACH DAY IS THE SAME. WORK, WORK HARDER, OR BE WHIPPED.

WHEN HARRIET WAS 12, SHE STARTED TO WORK IN THE FIELDS. THE WORK WAS TIRING. THERE WAS LITTLE TIME TO REST.

HARRIET ALWAYS CARED ABOUT PEOPLE. WHEN SHE WAS 13, ANOTHER SLAVE TRIED TO RUN AWAY. HARRIET TRIED TO PROTECT THE MAN FROM THEIR **OVERSEER.**

HARRIET! ARE YOU HURT?

THE OVERSEER THREW A LARGE PIECE OF METAL AT THE MAN, BUT IT MISSED. INSTEAD, IT HIT HARRIET.

HARRIET, WAKE UP! WE HAVE TO GET BACK TO WORK NOW. THERE IS NO TIME TO WASTE.

THE BLOW INJURED HARRIET'S BRAIN. FOR THE REST OF HER LIFE, SHE WOULD SOMETIMES GO INTO A DEEP SLEEP WITHOUT ANY WARNING.

WHEN SHE WAS ABOUT 25, HARRIET MARRIED JOHN TUBMAN. JOHN WAS NOT A SLAVE. HE WAS FREE.

IN 1849, HARRIET'S MASTER DIED. SHE HEARD **RUMORS** THAT SHE WAS GOING TO BE SOLD TO ANOTHER MASTER.

THE MASTER HAS DIED. WHAT WILL HAPPEN TO US?

I HEAR WE WILL BE SOLD.

I MUST RUN AWAY, AND I MUST DO IT SOON.

HARRIET WAS AFRAID HER LIFE WOULD BECOME EVEN HARDER. SHE KNEW SHE MUST GO TO THE NORTH. SLAVERY WAS NOT LEGAL IN THE NORTH.

HARRIET AND HER BROTHERS RAN AWAY. HOWEVER, HER BROTHERS BECAME AFRAID. THEY WENT BACK TO THE PLANTATION.

WE HAVE DECIDED TO GO BACK.

IT IS TOO DANGEROUS TO GO ON. WE WILL GET CAUGHT.

HARRIET USED THE NORTH STAR TO TELL HER WHAT DIRECTION TO TRAVEL.

I WILL FOLLOW THAT STAR TO THE NORTH. I MUST TRAVEL BY NIGHT.

HARRIET WENT ON ALONE. SLAVE OWNERS OFFERED MONEY TO PEOPLE WHO CAUGHT RUNAWAY SLAVES. HARRIET KNEW THEY WOULD BE HUNTING HER.

IF I KEEP TRAVELING NORTH, I WILL SOON BE FREE. IF I GET CAUGHT, I WILL BE KILLED.

COME IN. YOU CAN REST HERE UNTIL TOMORROW NIGHT.

AT LAST, I AM FREE.

HARRIET USED THE UNDERGROUND RAILROAD TO ESCAPE. IT WAS A SERIES OF SECRET PATHS AND HIDING PLACES. ALONG THE WAY WERE "SAFE" HOUSES. PEOPLE WHO HELPED RUNAWAY SLAVES ESCAPE FROM SLAVERY LIVED IN THESE HOUSES.

HARRIET WENT ON, **TRUDGING** THROUGH THE NIGHTS. ONE DAY, AS THE SUN ROSE, SHE CROSSED THE **MASON-DIXON LINE**. SHE WAS IN THE NORTH. AT THAT MOMENT, HARRIET KNEW SHE HAD TO HELP OTHERS TO FREEDOM, TOO.

HARRIET NEVER FORGOT HOW SHE FELT WHEN SHE CROSSED THE MASON-DIXON LINE. SHE SPOKE OF THAT MOMENT MANY TIMES LATER IN LIFE.

WHEN I FOUND I HAD CROSSED THAT LINE, I LOOKED AT MY HANDS TO SEE IF I WAS THE SAME PERSON. THERE WAS SUCH GLORY OVER EVERYTHING, AND I FELT LIKE I WAS IN HEAVEN.

I WILL SAVE MY MONEY. I NEED IT TO GO BACK SOUTH AND RESCUE OTHERS.

AFTER SHE WAS FREE, HARRIET WENT TO PHILADELPHIA. SHE FOUND WORK COOKING AND CLEANING.

ONE YEAR AFTER SHE ESCAPED, HARRIET WENT BACK TO RESCUE HER SISTER AND HER SISTER'S CHILDREN. LATER, SHE BROUGHT SEVERAL OF HER BROTHERS TO THE NORTH.

HARRIET WENT TO GET HER HUSBAND ON HER THIRD TRIP. HOWEVER, HE HAD MARRIED ANOTHER WOMAN. SO SHE FOUND OTHERS WHO WANTED TO GO NORTH.

COME WITH ME, AND YOU WILL HAVE A BETTER LIFE.

SOON, HARRIET BECAME KNOWN AS A "CONDUCTOR" ON THE UNDERGROUND RAILROAD.

THE SOUTHERN PLANTATION OWNERS KNEW ABOUT HARRIET, TOO. THEY OFFERED $40,000 TO ANYONE WHO CAPTURED HER.

WHEN SHE MADE TRIPS SOUTH, HARRIET OFTEN **DISGUISED** HERSELF. ONE TIME SHE RAN INTO A FORMER MASTER ON THE STREET. HE DID NOT EVEN RECOGNIZE HER.

SOMETIMES HARRIET STOLE A MASTER'S **BUGGY.** SHE WOULD HIDE THE RUNAWAY SLAVES IN IT.

NO MATTER WHAT HAPPENS OR WHAT YOU HEAR, YOU MUST LIE STILL AND NOT MAKE A SOUND.

HAVE THE BABY DRINK THIS. THEN SHE WILL BE QUIET.

HARRIET KNEW A CRYING BABY COULD GIVE THEM AWAY. SHE CARRIED MEDICINE TO MAKE BABIES SLEEP.

HARRIET KNEW THAT IF ANY OF THE RUNAWAYS TURNED BACK, THEY WOULD BE CAPTURED AND BEATEN. THEY MIGHT BE FORCED TO TELL THE SECRETS OF THE UNDERGROUND RAILROAD.

YOU CANNOT TURN BACK NOW. NO MATTER WHAT, YOU MUST CONTINUE.

AS A CONDUCTOR ON THE UNDERGROUND RAILROAD, HARRIET HELPED HUNDREDS OF ENSLAVED PEOPLE TRAVEL TO FREEDOM. EACH TIME SHE RETURNED TO THE SOUTH, SHE PUT HER LIFE IN DANGER.

WE MADE IT TO THE NORTH. YOU ARE NOW IN THE STATE OF PENNSYLVANIA, SO YOU ARE FREE!

HERE IS SOME WARM SOUP AND BREAD. YOU ARE SAFE HERE.

OVER 10 YEARS, HARRIET MADE 19 TRIPS TO THE SOUTH.

HARRIET TUBMAN IS JUST LIKE MOSES. IN THE BIBLE, MOSES LED HIS PEOPLE TO FREEDOM. HARRIET HAS LED US TO FREEDOM.

HARRIET ALSO WENT TO ANTISLAVERY MEETINGS. SHE MADE FRIENDS WITH MANY OTHER ABOLITIONISTS.

WE WILL OVERTHROW **PREJUDICE** WITH THE POWER OF LOVE.

FREDERICK DOUGLASS WAS A FAMOUS BLACK ABOLITIONIST. HE FOUGHT AGAINST SLAVERY. DOUGLASS GREATLY ADMIRED HARRIET.

YOU HAVE GONE THROUGH GREAT DANGER TO HELP OUR PEOPLE.

IN ALL MY JOURNEYS, I NEVER LOST A PASSENGER.

WHEN THE CIVIL WAR STARTED, HARRIET WANTED TO HELP. SHE UNDERSTOOD THAT THE **UNION** MUST WIN THE WAR IN ORDER FOR ALL SLAVES TO BE FREED.

EATING THIS FOOD WILL HELP KEEP YOU STRONG. THERE IS WORK AHEAD.

LATER IN THE CIVIL WAR, HARRIET BECAME A UNION SPY. SHE HELPED MAKE A PLAN TO FREE SLAVES WHO LIVED ALONG A RIVER IN SOUTH CAROLINA. SHE FOUND OUT WHERE **CONFEDERATE** SOLDIERS WERE HIDING.

THERE ARE SOLDIERS ALONG THE RIVERBANK AT THIS SPOT.

THE LEADER OF THE UNION ARMY IN THIS AREA WAS COLONEL JAMES MONTGOMERY. ON JUNE 1, 1863, HIS SOLDIERS TOOK THREE **GUNBOATS** ALONG THE RIVER.

WHEN DAWN CAME, THE UNION SOLDIERS ATTACKED THE SOUTHERN PLANTATIONS. THEY BURNED MANY BUILDINGS.

WE ARE BLOWING UP THE BRIDGE SO THAT IT WILL BE HARDER FOR THE CONFEDERATE ARMY TO GET SUPPLIES.

AT FIRST, WHEN THE SLAVES SAW THE BOATS, THEY WERE AFRAID. THEN THEY FOUND OUT THE SOLDIERS HAD COME TO FREE THEM. THEY RAN AND JUMPED ON THE BOATS.

HURRY. WE MUST GET ON THE BOATS NOW.

I AM NOT GOING TO BE LEFT BEHIND!

THE BOATS CARRIED THE SLAVES TO FREEDOM. IN ALL, ABOUT 750 SLAVES WERE FREED.

WHEN THE CIVIL WAR WAS OVER, HARRIET HELPED CARE FOR THE SICK AND WOUNDED.

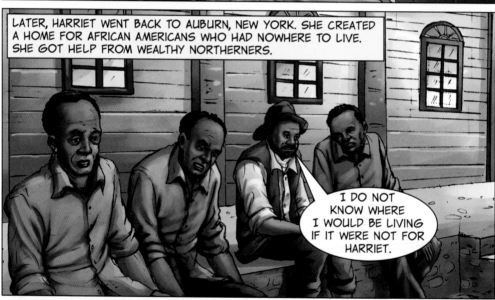

LATER, HARRIET WENT BACK TO AUBURN, NEW YORK. SHE CREATED A HOME FOR AFRICAN AMERICANS WHO HAD NOWHERE TO LIVE. SHE GOT HELP FROM WEALTHY NORTHERNERS.

I DO NOT KNOW WHERE I WOULD BE LIVING IF IT WERE NOT FOR HARRIET.

HARRIET ALSO STARTED SEVERAL SCHOOLS.

GETTING A GOOD EDUCATION WILL HELP YOU DO WELL IN THE FUTURE.

HARRIET LIVED TO BE 93. FROM A YOUNG AGE, HARRIET KNEW SHE HAD TO BE FREE. SHE ALSO KNEW THAT SHE HAD TO HELP OTHERS TO FREEDOM.

THERE'S TWO THINGS I GOT A RIGHT TO AND THESE ARE DEATH AND LIBERTY. IF I COULD NOT HAVE ONE, I WOULD HAVE THE OTHER.

HARRIET TUBMAN
1820-1913

THE "MOSES OF HER PEOPLE." HARRIET TUBMAN OF THE BUCKTOWN DISTRICT FOUND FREEDOM FOR HERSELF AND SOME THREE HUNDRED OTHER SLAVES WHOM SHE LED NORTH. IN THE CIVIL WAR SHE SERVED THE UNION ARMY AS A NURSE, SCOUT AND SPY.

MARYLAND CIVIL WAR CENTENNIAL COMMISSION

TODAY, HARRIET TUBMAN IS REMEMBERED AS SOMEONE WHO CARED ABOUT THE POOR, THE SICK, AND EVERYONE WHO WANTED TO BE FREE.

Timeline

Mid-1700s	Harriet's ancestors arrive in America from Africa to be sold as slaves.
About 1820	Harriet is born.
About 1826	Edward Brodas loans out Harriet to work on a nearby plantation.
About 1832	Harriet begins working in the fields.
About 1833	Harriet is injured when she tries to help another slave.
1844	Harriet marries John Tubman.
1849	Harriet escapes to the North.
1850	Harriet helps her sister escape to the North.
1851	Harriet helps a brother escape to the North.
1853	Harriet helps three more brothers escape from slavery.
1857	Harriet brings her elderly parents to the North.
1863	Harriet serves as a spy for the Union Army.
1865	Harriet works to take care of African American soldiers who have been wounded in the Civil War.
1868	Harriet cares for elderly and homeless African American people in her home.
1913	At about age 93, Harriet dies.

Glossary

abolitionist (a-buh-LIH-shun-ist) Person who worked to end slavery.

ancestors (AN-ses-terz) Relatives who lived long ago.

buggy (BUH-gee) A small cart for short transportations of heavy materials.

conductors (kun-DUK-terz) People who helped guide slaves to freedom on the Underground Railroad.

Confederate (kun-FEH-duh-ret) Relating to a person who fought for the South in the Civil War.

disgrace (dis-GRAYS) Something done that other people disapprove of.

disguised (dis-GYZD) Wore a costume or an outfit to hide one's identity.

gunboats (GUN-bohts) Small lightly armed ships that were used in shallow waters.

Mason-Dixon Line (MAY-suhn DIK-sun LYN) An imaginary line that divided the Northern states (the Union) and the Southern states (the Confederacy).

overseer (OH-ver-see-ur) A person who watches over workers.

plantation (plan-TAY-shun) A very large farm where crops are grown.

prejudice (PREH-juh-dis) Disliking a group of people different from you.

rumors (ROO-murs) Stories that are heard by people with no proof that the stories are true.

trudging (TRUJ-ing) Walking or marching steadily and usually with much effort.

Underground Railroad (UN-dur-grownd RAYL-rohd) A system set up to help slaves move to freedom in the North.

Union (YOON-yun) The Northern states that stayed with the national government during the Civil War.

Index

A
abolitionists, 16
Auburn, New York, 13, 20

B
Brodas, Edward, 5

C
Civil War, 17, 18, 19, 20, 21
Confederate Army, 18, 19

D
Douglass, Frederick, 3, 16

G
Greene, Harriet, 3, 4, 5, 6, 13

M
Maryland, 4, 21
Mason-Dixon Line, 11
Montgomery, James, 18
Moses, 16, 21

N
North Star, 10
nursing, 20, 21

P
Pennsylvania, 12, 15
plantation life, 5, 6, 7, 8, 9, 12, 13

R
Ross, Benjamin, 3, 5, 13

S
safe houses, 3, 11, 15
slave life, 4, 5, 6, 7, 8, 9, 12, 13
South Carolina, 18
spying, 18, 21

T
Tubman, John, 9, 12

U
Underground Railroad, 3, 11,
    13, 14, 15, 16
Union Army, 17, 18, 19, 21

Websites

Due to the changing nature of Internet links, PowerKids Press has developed an online list of websites related to the subject of this book. This site is updated regularly. Please use this link to access the list:

www.powerkidslinks.com/jgaah/tubman/